MW01626989

ODYSSEYS OF PETER SÍS

The Eric Carle Museum of Picture Book Art

Amherst, Massachusetts

June 8 – October 27, 2019

This catalog has been published in conjunction with the exhibition *The Picture Book Odysseys of Peter Sís*.

ISBN 978-1-59288-042-3

Catalog design by Rita Marshall
Printed in Italy
First Edition

The Carle is deeply proud to be the organizer of *The Picture Book Odysseys of Peter Sís,* an exhibition that pays tribute to the irrepressible energy of Peter Sís and his art. His curiosity about the world—the way he mines its complicated history and the human drive—has informed every mark of his pen. Many of his artistic impulses are also a clear reflection of his own outsized life story and experience.

Though Peter has published widely in newspapers, magazines, and books, Ellen Keiter, The Carle's chief curator, has chosen to focus the exhibition on Peter's output of meticulously detailed children's books that form his central body of work. Her challenge has been to capture the essence of a picture-book artist whose imagination ranges from the heart-soaring to the heartbreaking. Each illustration contains a world unto itself, beckoning children to be his co-conspirators in the unveiling of a story, layer by layer.

For *Picture Book Odysseys*, Ellen chose illustrations from 26 picture books. The presentation also includes examples of Peter's wide ranging and playful forays into everything from painted eggs to subway murals. (My personal favorites on view are his notebooks—part sketchbook, research notebook, and scrapbook. Peter creates one for each book project. He says they contain some of his favorite drawings, full of all the raw emotion and excitement of working through a story.) Peter has won some

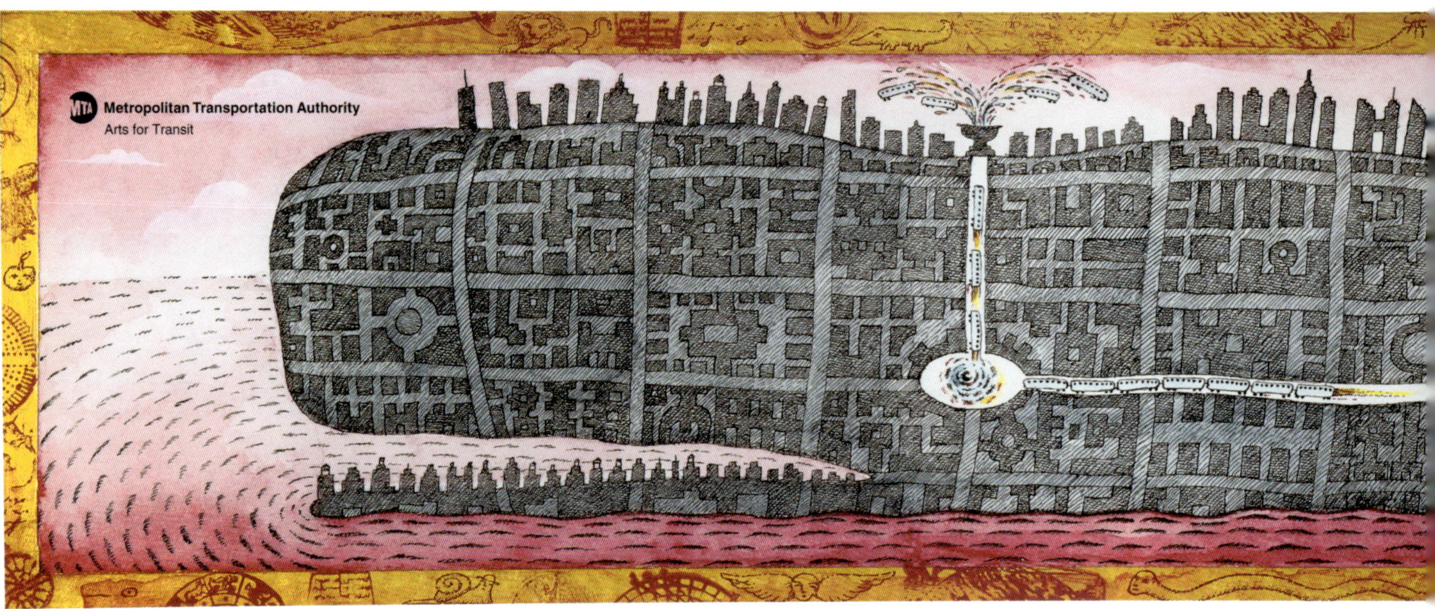

of the field's highest accolades—a Hans Christian Andersen Award, a MacArthur Fellowship—but as every reader of his knows, his work speaks for itself.

Ellen and I want to thank Peter and his wife, the filmmaker Terry Lajtha, for their help and kindness throughout the planning of this exhibition, and for their loan of art. Macmillan Children's Publishing Group has generously underwritten the exhibition. Our deepest thanks to Jonathan Yaged and all of the talented team at Macmillan. Our gratitude as well to Brenda Bowen, Peter's literary agent—another good friend to The Carle. Finally, we want to acknowledge Andrew Lass, professor emeritus at Mount Holyoke College and scholar of Czech culture, who wrote the beautiful foreword and encouraged us throughout the long curation process. When he and Peter met here at The Carle some years ago, they discovered in an instant a shared history of growing up in former Czechoslovakia, and a new and important friendship.

To Ellen and her team, and all of the staff at The Carle—thank you for your creativity and dedication. To Eric Carle, another big admirer of Peter's work, *děkuji!* We are so proud to champion the art of children's books.

Alexandra Kennedy
Executive Director
The Eric Carle Museum of Picture Book Art

Manhattan Whale, poster design commissioned by Arts for Transit, Metropolitan Transportation Authority, New York City, 2001

ON LEARNING HOW TO FLY WITH PETER SÍS

BY ANDY LASS

Professor Emeritus, Mount Holyoke College

Dagmar and Václav Havel VISION 97 laureate

Peter and I first met in the spring of 2014 in the back of The Eric Carle Museum's great concourse, at the corner right across from the library. Peter was in town to give the annual BERL lecture and sign lots of books, I came to meet Peter (and give him a volume of my poetry). After being introduced by Alix Kennedy, we switched to Czech, which turned out to be a Prague argot. It took but a few sentences to figure out that we must have sat near each other at one of the establishment defying Prague music venues that marked the way, in the mid-1960s, to what became known as the Prague Spring of 1968. A Slovak rock group, The Beatmen, was playing on the stage of the renowned Spejbl & Hurvínek puppet theatre. I sat next to my friend, the visiting American Beat poet Allen Ginsberg. Not to be undone, the secret police used this opportunity to steal his precious journal. Thereby hangs a longer story about the rebellious significance of poetry and music, long hair, blue jeans, American cigarettes, Western cinema or the theatre of the absurd, in the battle of true meaning against propaganda. The one event among the many that sufficed to establish that, while Peter and I had not met before, we had been together most of our lives.

As our ensuing friendship, best described as enigmatic realism, continues to flower, its roots keep growing thicker into the past. We came of age together, amidst a battle that defined our lives and those of others, in the pursuit of freedom at a time when the long communist winter began to thaw—it lasted several years, the best years of our lives—until the Spring was cut short on the night of August 21, 1968 when Soviet military transport planes loaded with tanks landed in Prague, with an order to halt the contagious sense of incredible lightness that we shared, in order to fix the crumbling Wall. Oppressors operate in many ways, and walls of lies are their favorite tool. Most everyone chocks, eventually. Many are killed, while a few get out.

We both grew up in Prague as outsiders. I arrived from New York City, Peter from Brno, the capital of Moravia, as kids, not long after the end of World War II. As young adults, our lives interrupted, I got myself kicked out of Czechoslovakia in the 1970s, Peter traveled West in the mid-1980s. Like so many others, we managed to get out of the walled-in world, but we never got the world that we called home out of us. Here is a sampling of trivia we have unearthed so far (the past has no bottom) that bind a friendship both fortuitous and foretold:

We can remember wearing our obligatory pioneer red scarfs to school where we were taught to read and write and count colorful buttons and learn about the Soviet Union where

"tomorrow means yesterday" and one day, under advance communism, there will be no need for money, and joined in singing "we shall command the winds and the rains" (and grow oranges in Siberia).

We spent hours in bed nursing colds (or pretending to), leafing through our favorite books, among them "The World in Pictures" (*Orbis Pictus*, 1658), with its intricate engravings depicting book making, by Johannes Amos Comenius. This pioneering work in picture books and modern pedagogy continues to hold a very special place for both of us. The Moravian Reform philosopher and teacher escaped the Counter Reformation to Amsterdam as if to presage the culture of exile and erasure that is Central Europe, and whom we were meant to be when we grew up. And so it would be. One picture book artist and one pedagogue.

Like other kids we learned to play marbles and, eventually, ride a bike, but Peter also dressed up as Robinson Crusoe while I whacked my Water Spirit and Silly Hans marionettes around, in a theatre my dad built from old crates (I also planted some brussels sprouts in a bed of mashed potatoes on the dramatically lit stage). And like most of our friends and their parents, but not all, we learned to suspect what we did not fully understand, that in this Promised Land what was not mandatory was not allowed and that, in fact, yesterday continued to be tomorrow. That freedom was not unlike Robinson's island, built on trust that fosters respect and rewards us with intimacy, that you must persist beyond the dream, whether yours or your parents or that of Václav Havel, Nelson Mandela or Martin Luther King, and like Homer's Odysseus

Peter Sís (right) and Andy Lass (left)

engage your imagination and work your way through the Underground, that the Arts were among the most potent vehicles of freedom and that joining in on the struggle was not heroic, just attractive in all senses of the word.

I can still recall the sigh of relief we felt (laughing) when, in the early '60s, after the annual May 9th end of WWII military parade–oh how we admired those polished tanks and military transporters rattling over the cobble stones–as the last Soviet built Mig aircraft broke the sound barrier and finally disappeared, the crowds gathered in front of the tribune. It was a tense moment when, from the Politburo's line-up President Monkey (that was his nickname) made the following important announcement: "comrades, there shall be meat, yes comrades, meat, there shall be meat."

I had dropped out of high school (for a year) so I spent my time hanging out with my friend Jiří Stivín, the budding jazz musician and wind instrument prodigy. We returned to his apartment very late, after the jazz club closed. His mother was playing solitaire in the front room while Jiří continued to blow his horns (to the dismay and anger of the sleep deprived neighbors) with Rahsaan Rolland Kirk playing from the record player in the background. I fiddled around in the once bathroom now darkroom developing my first prints. If I had known that Peter had used that very bathtub for its original purpose years earlier, before his father had exchanged apartments with Stivín, what difference would it have made? Years later, long before I met Peter, I met Peter's father, at a first screening of a documentary he had made of the renowned

"Everyone wanted to draw," *The Wall: Growing Up Behind the Iron Curtain* (Frances Foster Books, 2007)

baritone (and my adoring African-American uncle) Aubrey Pankey who lived in East Berlin at the time, and who would be murdered by the East German police a few years later.

Our parallel lives kept crossing paths, perhaps because all walls have corners where you can meet. Had we not met across from The Eric Carle Museum's library, we were already meant to meet through our mutual friend and Peter's Czech publisher Joachim Dvořák (Labyrint Press). Now we are three. Drawing and translating, writing and publishing books for children and picture book art.

Although the ugliest walls of Central Europe have since fallen and many others have been lovingly repaired (or at least whitewashed), creepy walls keep showing up in all corners of the Earth. Our past continues to breathe sense into the present, worried yes, but also hopeful as we breathe poetry into the landscapes Peter and I draw. We had learned to see in one way and not some other way. Peter's birds and flying figures soaring high continue to disclose unwelcome barriers, pointing the way and beyond. His stunning images show what I can only share in words or disclose in photographs, the infinite joy that comes from the freedom of speech, the freedom of assembly, and the freedom of movement, that the struggle never ends, that it can hurt and that life can be convoluted and inexplicable yet always worth it and worth that beautiful smile for that.

Thank you Peter for being our friend!

"They painted a wall filled with their dreams and repainted it again and again," *The Wall: Growing Up Behind the Iron Curtain* (Frances Foster Books, 2007)

"It was the Prague Spring of 1968!" ***The Wall: Growing Up Behind the Iron Curtain*** (Frances Foster Books, 2007)

JOURNEY: PETER SÍS'S LIFE IN PICTURES

BY ELLEN KEITER
Chief Curator
The Eric Carle Museum of Picture Book Art

Peter Sís's books for children chart the journeys, both real and imagined, that define the human experience. "The connecting thing in all my books is the fact that somebody's dreaming about places or searching for someplace or going places," he says.[1] Sís's stories are fueled by his memories growing up in Czechoslovakia under an oppressive communist regime, but also by his filmmaker father who travelled the world and told him mysterious tales of the strange places he had seen. Sís celebrates the daring adventurers and inquisitive scientists who challenged accepted beliefs, even at their own peril. Whether portraying extraordinary real-life expeditions or literary flights of fantasy, Sís's books embody the principles of freedom and celebrate artistic expression, independent thought, and the autonomy to transcend borders, physical and political.

"As long as he could remember, he had loved to draw," begins his picture-book autobiography *The Wall: Growing Up Behind the Iron Curtain* (2007). Born in Brno, Czechoslovakia in 1949, Sís's formative years and early career came at the height of the Cold War and Soviet totalitarianism. While his artist parents encouraged his creativity at home, Sís was careful what he drew or said in school. In *The Wall,* red flags, red stars, and red hammers and sickles puncture the black-and-white illustrations of his childhood. "This was the time of brainwashing," he writes at the bottom of a double-page spread depicting Joseph Stalin riding a red wave of military might. Sís portrays the omnipresent secret police as pigs who read mail, enforce dress codes, and encourage residents to spy on their neighbors.

Sís's family had spent time abroad and acquainted him with the larger world. His grandfather, who helped design the train stations in Cleveland and Chicago in the 1930s, shared comic strips saved from the *Chicago Tribune*—Little Orphan Annie, Mutt and Jeff, and Krazy Kat. His father, who filmed documentaries in England, France, Greece, Indonesia, and Tibet, returned from trips with magical stories about poetry and jazz, Elvis and the Rolling Stones.

Life blossomed for Sís during the Prague Spring of 1968, a brief period of political and cultural liberation. Censorship was lifted and the arts were celebrated. "Prague Spring was the best time of my life," he recalls. "We could play rock music and stage avant-garde theatre, grow long hair, draw Beatles, and travel outside the country."[2] Sís, who loved music, formed a band and became a DJ with his own radio program. He conveys the joy of artistic freedom in *The Wall* with a composition that explodes with psychedelic colors and '60s symbolism.

"Then—it was all over," he writes. The Curtain descended again as 500,000 communist troops overtook the city.

Sketchbook pages for *The Wall: Growing Up Behind the Iron Curtain* (Frances Foster Books, 2007)

NIGHT OF AUGUST 20-1968
One night - Big Surprise

“He dreamed of being free,” ***The Wall: Growing Up Behind the Iron Curtain*** (Frances Foster Books, 2007)

"Sometimes dreams come true," ***The Wall: Growing Up Behind the Iron Curtain*** (Frances Foster Books, 2007)

Sís's pages revert to black-and-white. "It's not just that the world now appeared colorless to us," Sís says, "it's that we felt caged in—the opposite of the unbearable lightness of being."[3] Sís illustrates the imaginative ways he contemplated escape, whether tunneling underground, pole vaulting over barbed wire barriers, or inventing a flying bicycle to carry him to freedom. In the book's final illustration, the Berlin Wall crumbles and the red sky fades to deep blue: "Sometimes dreams come true."

Sís graduated from the Academy of Applied Arts in Prague where he studied with the acclaimed illustrator and animator Jiří Trnka. He was offered an assistant professor position at the Academy—the youngest teacher ever—under the condition he join the communist party. He refused. Trying to obtain permission to have his own studio, he was told only "socialist realists" approved by the government could have one. Without a full-time job or a studio, Sís painted whatever he could, including the chairs, light switches, and refrigerator in his home. His first professional assignment, to design a record album cover, was subject to censorship—as was all art of the time—and scoured for secret meanings. Animated film seemed a safer and more creative venture, and interest in Sís's first film, *Island for 6,000 Alarm Clocks* (1977), made it possible for him to study in England with Quentin Blake at The Royal College of Art. In 1980, Sís's film *Heads* won the Berlin Film Festival Golden Bear award, which opened the door to the western world. He worked on a TV series in Switzerland, *Hexe Lakritze* (1981), and *Players* (1982) in London, which were both based on his illustrations.

Film also brought Sís to America. The government sent him to Los Angeles in 1982 to work on an animated film about Czechoslovakia for the 1984 summer Olympics. When the Soviet bloc countries boycotted the games, Sís was ordered back to Prague. Ambivalent and tortured, not knowing if he would ever be allowed to return to his family or country, he decided to remain in America.

Earning money to support himself proved difficult. Sís painted enigmatic faces and miniature landscapes on goose eggs that he sold for $50 apiece. He earned a commission for his mesmerizing portrait on the movie poster *Amadeus*, the 1984 Oscar-winning film directed by fellow Czech Milös Forman. The assignment allowed him to purchase an old car. The curator of the Municipal Art Museum in Los Angeles, Josine Ianco, mailed photocopies of Sís's work to Maurice Sendak. The American master was intrigued and called Sís collect from New York. His recommendation was resolute: he would help Sís enter the field of children's books, but he had to get out of California ("Hollywood is the worst place! Do you like Reagan?" Sís amusingly recalls him saying). Sís acknowledges he wasn't quite aware of who Sendak was at the time—nor did he know much about American children's books—but the phone call changed his life.

Soon after, Sís packed his banged-up Mustang convertible and headed east. Ready for adventure, but without a map (strange for an artist who often includes maps in his books), he presumed if he drove straight east he would arrive in New York. Instead, he found himself in San Antonio, Texas, where he finally asked a policeman for directions. Once in Manhattan, he stayed in a friend's basement apartment and assembled a portfolio. He

visited one publisher after another, not knowing whether to work for *Time* magazine or *High Times* magazine. An editor at *Esquire* was the first to print one of Sís's drawings, for which he was paid $600.

Sís eventually landed at *The New York Times*, where he would contribute more than 1,000 illustrations over 18 years. He worked closely with the *Times*' art director Steven Heller. Sís called every Wednesday morning at nine to learn if he had an assignment for the week. Drawings for the Op-Ed page were due within 24 hours, illustrations for the Book Review in four days. Sís went in person to pick up the articles and manuscripts at the *Times* offices, often returning with the illustration the next day, after staying up and drawing all night.

As an immigrant, Sís felt a need to prove himself. He developed a unique style of meticulous stippled ink dots to define his compositions. It is this delicate, pointillist approach that remains a hallmark of Sís's art. He says, "... I had a very time-consuming style which I invented in order to be very special, but it completely killed any free time, or any weekends. I think I'm sort of very lucky that I even found my wife!"[4] He once spent three days crisscrossing a single illustration in *The Three Golden Keys* (1994). Despite the self-imposed regimen, Sís acknowledges, "It can be physically painful, but then when you see the beautiful picture in the end ... you know it's special what you have done."[5]

"I follow the determined cat back across the ancient bridge," *The Three Golden Keys* (Doubleday, 1994)

"They told one another stories, and they took long walks together," ***Rainbow Rhino*** (Alfred A. Knopf, 1987)

"Then, on the seventy-first day, a little piece of land appeared on the horizon," ***Follow the Dream: The Story of Christopher Columbus*** (Alfred A. Knopf, 1991)

Sís's first forays into children's books were as an illustrator for other authors. He made fine pen-and-ink drawings for George Shannon's *Bean Boy* (1984) and Sid Fleischman's *The Whipping Boy* (1986), which won the Newbery Medal. Sís created his first children's picture book, *Rainbow Rhino*, in 1987. Several publishing houses initially turned down the project, considering the fable about a rhinoceros and his three colorful bird friends as esoteric and "too European." Editor Frances Foster at Alfred A. Knopf accepted the book, marking the beginning of a fruitful, 27-year partnership with Sís. He credits Foster with giving him "a chance to dare." *Rainbow Rhino*'s simple allegory and ethereal illustrations introduced Sís's work to a new audience of librarians, teachers, and young readers. *The New York Times* designated it one of the best illustrated children's books of the year.

Sís next created the early-reader counting books *Waving* (1988) and *Going Up* (1989), the playful *Beach Ball* (1990), and then, in a distinct turn, 1991's *Follow the Dream: The Story of Christopher Columbus*, the first of Sís's books about explorers and dreamers. Seeing now the devastating consequences of European colonialism and the fundamental issue with his subject, Sís reflects: "I grew up with the myth of Columbus's voyage ... I thought I had found a perfect explorer in him. Someone who was determined

"Massachusetts," *The Train of States* (Greenwillow Books, 2004)

to find the way, just like me."[6]

In response to the complexity of *Follow the Dream*, Sís's ensuing book was about a lonely and endangered creature. *An Ocean World* (1992) is a beautiful, nearly wordless story of a whale's quest for companionship after release from captivity. Although inspired by an article Sís read in the newspaper, the whale's journey is a metaphor for his own: freedom from confinement and the search for a new home. *Rainbow Rhino* and *An Ocean World* both present sequential panels to suggest the passage of time. It is a construct Sís would return to again, and with increasing sophistication.

Sís married documentary film editor Terry Lajtha in 1990. The birth of their children Madeleine and Matej inspired a new style and a series of early readers for the artist. In quick succession came *Fire Truck* (1998), *Trucks, Trucks, Trucks* (1999), *Ship Ahoy!* (1999), and *Dinosaur!* (2000). Sís conveys these simple stories in a clear graphic style defined by bold outlines, ample white space, and flat, unmodulated colors. They are also where Sís began to experiment with dramatic page folds. *The Train of States* (2004) and *Play, Mozart, Play!* (2006) are unique hybrids in which Sís combines the brighter palette and graphic sensibility of his early readers with the refined pointillism and shifting perspectives of his adventure biographies.

Published five years after the fall of the Berlin Wall, *The Three*

"Mozart played for kings and princes and dukes, and queens and one empress and one pope," ***Play, Mozart, Play!*** (Greenwillow Books, 2006)

Detail of illustration for *An Ocean World* (Greenwillow Books, 1992)

Golden Keys (1994) is a stunning, surreal return to Sís's childhood in Prague. The story is a modern-day fairytale that captures the beauty of the ancient city, meticulously rendered in oil pastel on gesso to simulate Renaissance frescos. A black cat with magic eyes leads readers through deserted streets inhabited only by Sís's memories. His tour-de-force map is an ornate urban maze of winding streets that delineate a hidden feline form. Readers journey to Prague's famous landmarks—the Klementinum Library, the Charles Bridge, and the Astronomical Clock—each revealing a Czech legend and a golden key. The three keys unlock the door to Sís's family home, a pulsating scarlet interior where "everything comes alive."

Sís dedicated the book to his daughter Madeleine so that one day she would "know where her father came from." Jacqueline Onassis, his editor at Doubleday, was so moved by Sís's story that she decided not to limit it to the prescribed 32-pages of a picture book and marketed *The Three Golden Keys* to both children and adults. It was the final book Onassis published before her death.

Madlenka (2000) is a story inspired by the multicultural neighborhood where Sís and his family lived. The book follows Madlenka (his daughter Madeleine) around a New York City block, which becomes a symbolic journey around the world. With the mind-bending precision of an M.C. Escher illustration, Sís constructs amazing birds-eye and tunnel-view perspectives of Madlenka's neighborhood. His innovative die-cut windows open to vivid, double-page spreads representing such countries as France, Germany, India, and China. Sís presents New York as a city of immigrants: "I wanted to show how wonderful life is here,"

"France," Madlenka (Frances Foster Books, 2000)

"Hey everyone...my tooth is loose!" *Madlenka* (Frances Foster Books, 2000)

Illustration for *Madlenka's Dog* (Frances Foster Books, 2002)

"He stumbled into a red room...," ***Tibet: Through the Red Box*** (Frances Foster Books, 1998)

he says, "because I came from a country where everybody and everything looked the same."[7] He made two sequels, *Madlenka's Dog* (2002) and *Madlenka Soccer Star* (2010).

Legendary explorers and scientists who personify the quest for truth are another literary inspiration for Sís. A fascination with the heroic journey came early for him. When Sís was four years old, his father Vladimir was drafted into the army film unit and sent to China to record the construction of a highway in a remote western province, which he later discovered was Tibet. Sís's *Tibet through the Red Box* (1998) chronicles his father's nearly two-year odyssey wandering the Himalaya Mountains after a landslide stranded him from his crew. Lost without a map, "traveling into the unknown," he entered the forbidden city of Lhasa, where he met the 19-year-old Dalai Lama and warned him of China's covert plan to use the highway to launch an invasion.

Tibet through the Red Box recounts a mystical journey through a land of Yeti, yaks, monasteries, and creation legends. The narrator's voice alternates between Sís's childhood remembrances and his father's diary entries, which Sís faithfully recreates on faded, tea-stained colored papers. Throughout he includes symbolic paintings of his father's study, including the red box containing his travel journals on the desk. Vladimir's ghostly figure haunts family vignettes of Sís, his mother, and younger sister Hana.

Sís has created picture book biographies on the real-life voyages of Christopher Columbus, Charles Darwin, Antoine de Saint-Exupéry, and Czech folk hero Jan Welzl. He has also depicted

"I hear the deep voice of my father," *Tibet: Through the Red Box* (Frances Foster Books, 1998)

the life and persecution of Galileo Galilei. These are complex and heavily researched books with layered levels of access: family trees, timelines, and casts of historical figures coalesce to tell the stories. Nearly all include meticulous hand-drawn maps that chart the travels of the protagonists. Sís provides simple prose in Roman lettering for young readers; more advanced information is written in script for older audiences. He breaks the book's static orientation by swirling his text around pictures and along the peripheries of the page.

In *Starry Messenger* (1996), Sís chronicles the life of 17th-century Italian scientist, astronomer, and mathematician Galileo Galilei, who was found guilty of heresy in 1633 for challenging the belief that the earth was the center of the universe. Sís's striking inquisition scene depicts rows of red-robed cardinals bearing down on the elderly scientist. He says, "A lot of Galileo is really to do with life in Prague in the late 60's and '70's."[8] His ingenious endpapers bridge the centuries, one depicting Galileo gazing through a spyglass at the Tuscan night sky, the other of an individual looking through a telescope above the New York City skyline.

Sís is currently working on a new picture book (as yet untitled) about Britain's Sir Nicholas Winton, a London stockbroker turned humanitarian who saved 699 Jewish children from Czechoslovakia on the eve of World War II by arranging their

Cover illustration for ***Starry Messenger: Galileo Galilei*** (Frances Foster Books, 1996)

Sketchbook page for forthcoming book on Nicholas Winton (unfinished), 2018

safe passage to Britain. Sís renders such atrocities as Kristallnacht in stark black-and-white compositions, while his illustrations of children are presented in gentle washes of color.

Sís is proud that his books span countries and continents, with translations in many languages. The American Library Association awarded him Caldecott Honor medals for *Starry Messenger*, *Tibet Through the Red Box*, and *The Wall*. In 2003 he became the first children's book artist to be named a MacArthur Fellow (the "genius grant," as it's often known). In 2012, he won the Hans Christian Andersen Medal, the prestigious international award for lasting contributions to children's literature.

Sís published his first picture book for adults in 2011, *The Conference of the Birds*, an adaptation of the epic 12th-century Persian poem. It is a breathtakingly beautiful book in which the birds of the world alight on a perilous journey in search of a king, and discover spiritual enlightenment. Birds, and themes of flight,

Sketchbook pages for *The Conference of the Birds* (The Penguin Press, 2011)

figure in several of Sís's picture books. "The birds never needed passports," Sís recalls of his youth. "We always thought, the birds can go wherever they want, and we couldn't really. The birds were very much the symbol of ... free movement for me."[9] In December 2018, on Human Rights Day, Amnesty International unveiled a large tile mural in Lisbon, Portugal, depicting one of Sís's magnificent birds from *The Conference*.

Over the last seven years, Sís has partnered with Amnesty International's Art for Amnesty global artist engagement program on a series of commissioned tapestries in support of worldwide human rights. A team of talented artisans in Southern France weaves Sís's paintings into monumental tapestries that now don bustling public spaces. Sís's 24-foot tapestry honoring John Lennon, *Yellow Submarine*, is at the Ellis Island National Museum of Immigration. His memorial tapestry to Czech Republic President Václav Havel, *Flying Man*, is in Prague's Václav Havel Airport, and a commemorative tapestry of Nelson Mandela, titled *Flying Madiba*, is at the Cape Town International Airport. *Out of*

Illustration for *The Conference of the Birds* (The Penguin Press, 2011)

the Marvellous, Sís's tapestry representing the Irish poet Seamus Heaney, is displayed at Dublin Airport. Art for Amnesty recently commissioned Sís to portray pivotal events of the Civil Rights Movement—John Lewis and the 1961 Freedom Riders, Martin Luther King Jr.'s 1963 "I Have a Dream" speech, and the 1968 Memphis sanitation strike. The tapestries, with their flying motifs, were unveiled in 2017 at the Birmingham Civil Rights Institute in Alabama and are currently touring the U.S. "I don't know if anything like that will ever happen again," claims Sís, "but it's an incredible extension of my work in my life."[10]

Sís created two well-known artworks for the Metropolitan Transit Authority's New York City subway system. *Happy City* (2004) consists of four glass mosaic murals permanently installed at the 86th street station. In 2001, two months after 9/11, the MTA installed Sís's now-iconic 'Manhattan Whale' poster throughout the city's buses and subway cars. His playful take on New York's

"Dr. Darwin wants the best for his children," ***The Tree of Life: A Book Depicting the Life of Charles Darwin, Naturalist, Geologist, & Thinker*** (Frances Foster Books, 2003)

famous street grid proved a welcome sight for commuters in a city mired in despair and fear. The silhouette of the Twin Towers, drawn on the whale's forehead, became a poignant tribute.

Sís's personal life story and pursuit of freedom nourish his commitment to public art and bookmaking. Over a 30-year career in children's literature, he has invited readers of all ages to join him on incredible journeys. In accepting the Hans Christian Andersen Award, Sís reflected on his life as an author and illustrator: "I found out that one doesn't have to discover new continents, that people can explore in their mind even when locked in a prison cell and that books can be my home, my language, my country. I can share with my children and children of the world the universe of dreamers, seekers and people who dared to think differently."[11]

"When Charles is nine, his father sends him to join his brother at the nearby boarding school," *The Tree of Life: A Book Depicting the Life of Charles Darwin, Naturalist, Geologist, & Thinker* (Frances Foster Books, 2003)

"I hear voices, as in a dream," ***A Small Tall Tale from the Far Far North*** (Alfred A. Knopf, 1993)

"The Voyage of The Beagle," ***The Tree of Life: A Book Depicting the Life of Charles Darwin, Naturalist, Geologist, & Thinker*** (Frances Foster Books, 2003)

Illustration for *The Pilot and the Little Prince: The Life of Antoine de Saint-Exupéry* (Frances Foster Books, 2014)

"From the skies, Antoine watched the fires, smoke, and destruction the Germans left . . . ," *The Pilot and the Little Prince: The Life of Antoine de Saint-Exupéry* (Frances Foster Books, 2014)

ENDNOTES

1 NPR, "In 'Birds,' Sís Makes a Dream World for Grown-Ups," *NPR*, https://www.npr.org/2011/11/16/142396491/in-birds-sis-makes-a-dream-world-for-grown-ups (accessed 13 February 2019).

2 Peter Sís, "The Three Mentors," *International Board on Books for Young People*, http://www.ibby.org/subnavigation/archives/hans-christian-andersen-awards/2012/peter-sis/ (accessed 13 February 2019).

3 Peter Sís. Personal interview. April 2, 2018. Irvington, New York.

4 Reading Rockets, "Transcript of an Interview with Peter Sís," *Reading Rockets,* http://www.readingrockets.org/books/interviews/sis/transcript (accessed 13 February 2019).

5 NPR, op. cit., https://www.npr.org/2011/11/16/142396491/in-birds-sis-makes-a-dream-world-for-grown-ups.

6 Peter Sís, "My Life with Censorship," *Bookbird*, 2009, p. 45.

7 Carter Higgins, "Robinson + an interview with Peter Sís," Design of the Picture Book, http://www.designofthepicturebook.com/robinson-an-interview-with-peter-sis/ (accessed 13 February 2019).

8 CBS News. "Sís Stays in Touch with his Past," *CBS News*, https://www.cbsnews.com/news/sis-stays-in-touch-with-his-past/ (accessed 13 February 2019).

9 NPR, op. cit., https://www.npr.org/2011/11/16/142396491/in-birds-sis-makes-a-dream-world-for-grown-ups.

10 Ian Willoughby, "Peter Sís: Political Events are Giving My Stories about Parents and Children Fresh Meaning," *Radio Praha*, https://www.radio.cz/en/section/special/peter-sis-political-events-are-giving-my-stories-about-parents-and-children-fresh-meaning (accessed 13 February 2019).

11 Peter Sís, "The Three Mentors," op. cit., http://www.ibby.org/subnavigation/archives/hans-christian-andersen-awards/2012/peter-sis/.

"India," *Madlenka* (Frances Foster Books, 2000)

ILLUSTRATIONS

Unless otherwise noted, all illustrations by Peter Sís (American, born in Czechoslovakia, 1949) and courtesy of the artist.

Front cover: "Sick for a few weeks after getting lost in a snowstorm...." ***Tibet: Through the Red Box*** (Frances Foster Books). Pen and ink, watercolor, and gold leaf on paper. 17 x 17 inches. Copyright © 1998 Peter Sís. Reprinted with permission from Farrar, Straus, Giroux Books for Young Readers. All rights reserved.

Back cover: "There was nobody anywhere." ***The Three Golden Keys*** (Doubleday). Pen and ink, oil pastel, and gold leaf on paper. 13 x 21 inches. Copyright © 1994 Peter Sís.

Page 1: "He was tired in the Pope's court, and everyone could see the stars had left his eyes." ***Starry Messenger: Galileo Galilei*** (Frances Foster Books). Pen and ink and watercolor on paper. 11 x 13 inches. Copyright © 1996 Peter Sís. Reprinted with permission from Farrar, Straus, Giroux Books for Young Readers. All rights reserved.

Pages 2–3: "I invite them to my table and we celebrate the harvest." ***Robinson*** (Scholastic Press). Pen and ink and watercolor on paper. 12 x 20 inches. Copyright © 2017 Peter Sís. Courtesy of Scholastic Inc.

Pages 4–5: ***Manhattan Whale,*** poster design commissioned by Arts for Transit, Metropolitan Transportation Authority, New York City, 2001. Pen and ink, watercolor, and gold acrylic on paper. 8 x 43 inches. Copyright © Peter Sís.

Page 7: Peter Sís and Andy Lass. Photograph courtesy of Andy Lass.

Page 8: "Everyone wanted to draw." ***The Wall: Growing Up Behind the Iron Curtain*** (Frances Foster Books). Pen and black and red ink on paper. 14 x 10 inches. Copyright © 2007 Peter Sís. Reprinted with permission from Farrar, Straus, Giroux Books for Young Readers. All rights reserved.

Page 9: "They painted a wall filled with their dreams and repainted it again and again." ***The Wall: Growing Up Behind the Iron Curtain*** (Frances Foster Books). Pen and black and red ink on paper. 14 x 10 inches. Copyright © 2007 Peter Sís. Reprinted with permission from Farrar, Straus, Giroux Books for Young Readers. All rights reserved.

Page 10: "It was the Prague Spring of 1968!" ***The Wall: Growing Up Behind the Iron Curtain*** (Frances Foster Books). Pen and ink and watercolor on paper. 14 x 21 inches. Copyright © 2007 Peter Sís. Reprinted with permission from Farrar, Straus, Giroux Books for Young Readers. All rights reserved.

Pages 12–13: Sketchbook pages. ***The Wall: Growing Up Behind the Iron Curtain*** (Frances Foster Books). Pen and ink and colored pencil on paper. 12 x 18 inches (open). Copyright © 2007 Peter Sís. Reprinted with permission from Farrar, Straus, Giroux Books for Young Readers. All rights reserved.

Page 14: "He dreamed of being free." ***The Wall: Growing Up Behind the Iron Curtain*** (Frances Foster Books). Pen and ink and colored pencil on paper. 12 x 18 inches. Copyright © 2007 Peter Sís. Reprinted with permission from Farrar, Straus, Giroux Books for Young Readers. All rights reserved.

Page 15: "Sometimes dreams come true." ***The Wall: Growing Up Behind the Iron Curtain*** (Frances Foster Books). Pen and ink and watercolor on paper. 12 x 18 inches. Copyright © 2007 Peter Sís. Reprinted with permission from Farrar, Straus, Giroux Books for Young Readers. All rights reserved.

Page 17: "I follow the determined cat back across the ancient bridge." ***The Three Golden Keys*** (Doubleday). Pen and ink, oil pastel, and gold leaf on paper. 13 x 21 inches. Copyright © 1994 Peter Sís.

Page 18: "They told one another stories, and they took long walks together." ***Rainbow Rhino*** (Alfred A. Knopf). Pen and ink, oil pastel, and gesso on board. 11 x 16 inches. Copyright © 1987 Peter Sís.

Page 19: "Then, on the seventy-first day, a little piece of land appeared on the horizon." ***Follow the Dream: The Story of Christopher Columbus*** (Alfred A. Knopf). Pen and ink, oil pastel, gold leaf, and gesso on paper. 20 x 26 inches. Copyright © 1991 Peter Sís.

Page 20: "Massachusetts." ***The Train of States*** (Greenwillow Books). Pen and ink and watercolor on paper. 11 x 13 inches. Copyright © 2004 Peter Sís. Used by permission of HarperCollins Publishers.

Page 21: "Mozart played for kings and princes and dukes, and queens and one empress and one pope." ***Play, Mozart, Play!*** (Greenwillow Books). Pen and ink and watercolor on paper. 12 x 22 inches. Copyright © 2006 Peter Sís.

Pages 22–23: Illustration for page 17. ***An Ocean World*** (Greenwillow Books). Pen and ink and watercolor on paper. 11 x 15 inches. Copyright © 1992 Peter Sís. Used by permission of HarperCollins Publishers.

Page 24: "France." ***Madlenka*** (Frances Foster Books). Pen and ink and pastel on paper. 12 x 25 inches. Copyright © 2000 Peter Sís. Reprinted

with permission from Farrar, Straus, Giroux Books for Young Readers. All rights reserved.

Page 25: "Hey everyone…my tooth is loose!" ***Madlenka*** (Frances Foster Books). Pen and ink and watercolor on paper. 14 x 13 inches. Copyright © 2000 Peter Sís. Reprinted with permission from Farrar, Straus, Giroux Books for Young Readers. All rights reserved.

Pages 26–27: Illustration for pages 24–25. ***Madlenka's Dog*** (Frances Foster Books). Pen and ink and watercolor on paper. 9 x 19 inches. Copyright © 2002 Peter Sís. Reprinted with permission from Farrar, Straus, Giroux Books for Young Readers. All rights reserved.

Page 28: "He stumbled into a red room…." ***Tibet: Through the Red Box*** (Frances Foster Books). Pen and ink, watercolor, and gold leaf on paper. 16 x 16 inches. Copyright © 1998 Peter Sís. Reprinted with permission from Farrar, Straus, Giroux Books for Young Readers. All rights reserved.

Page 29: "I hear the deep voice of my father." ***Tibet: Through the Red Box*** (Frances Foster Books). Pen and ink, watercolor, gold acrylic, and gesso on paper. 10 x 20 inches. Copyright © 1998 Peter Sís. Reprinted with permission from Farrar, Straus, Giroux Books for Young Readers. All rights reserved.

Page 30: Cover illustration. ***Starry Messenger: Galileo Galilei*** (Frances Foster Books). Pen and ink and watercolor on paper. 13 x 20 inches. Copyright © 1996 Peter Sís. Reprinted with permission from Farrar, Straus, Giroux Books for Young Readers. All rights reserved.

Page 31: Sketchbook page for forthcoming book on Nicholas Winton (unfinished), 2019. Pen and ink and watercolor on paper. 12 x 9 inches (page). Copyright © Peter Sís.

Page 32: Sketchbook pages. ***The Conference of the Birds*** (The Penguin Press). Gesso and oil pastel on paper. 11 x 16 inches (open). Copyright © 2011 Peter Sís. Used by permission of Penguin Press, an imprint of Penguin Publishing Group, a division of Penguin Random House LLC. All rights reserved.

Page 33: Illustration for pages 64–65. ***The Conference of the Birds*** (The Penguin Press). Pen and ink on paper. 12 x 18 inches. Copyright © 2011 Peter Sís. Used by permission of Penguin Press, an imprint of Penguin Publishing Group, a division of Penguin Random House LLC. All rights reserved.

Page 34: "Dr. Darwin wants the best for his children." ***The Tree of Life: A Book Depicting the Life of Charles Darwin, Naturalist, Geologist, & Thinker*** (Frances Foster Books). Pen and ink and watercolor on paper. 11 x 13 inches. Copyright © 2003 Peter Sís. Reprinted with permission from Farrar, Straus, Giroux Books for Young Readers. All rights reserved.

Page 35: "When Charles is nine, his father send him to join his brother at the nearby boarding school." ***The Tree of Life: A Book Depicting the Life of Charles Darwin, Naturalist, Geologist, & Thinker*** (Frances Foster Books). Pen and ink and watercolor on paper. 10 x 10 inches. Copyright © 2003 Peter Sís. Reprinted with permission from Farrar, Straus, Giroux Books for Young Readers. All rights reserved.

Page 36: "I hear voices, as in a dream." ***A Small Tall Tale from the Far Far North*** (Alfred A. Knopf). Pen and ink and watercolor on paper. 9 x 21 inches. Copyright © 1993 Peter Sís.

Page 37: "The Voyage of The Beagle." ***The Tree of Life: A Book Depicting the Life of Charles Darwin, Naturalist, Geologist, & Thinker*** (Frances Foster Books). Pen and ink and watercolor on paper. 14 x 21 inches. Copyright © 2003 Peter Sís. Reprinted with permission from Farrar, Straus, Giroux Books for Young Readers. All rights reserved.

Page 38: Illustration for pages 16–17. ***The Pilot and the Little Prince: The Life of Antoine de Saint-Exupéry*** (Frances Foster Books). Pen

"Float," ***Ballerina!*** (Greenwillow Books, 2001)

and ink and watercolor on paper. 13 x 19 inches. Copyright © 2014 Peter Sís. Reprinted with permission from Farrar, Straus, Giroux Books for Young Readers. All rights reserved.

Page 39: "From the skies, Antoine watched the fires, smoke, and destruction the Germans left...." ***The Pilot and the Little Prince: The Life of Antoine de Saint-Exupéry*** (Frances Foster Books). Pen and ink and watercolor on paper. 12 x 18 inches. Copyright © 2014 Peter Sís. Reprinted with permission from Farrar, Straus, Giroux Books for Young Readers. All rights reserved.

Page 40: "India." ***Madlenka*** (Frances Foster Books). Pen and ink, watercolor, and gold acrylic on paper. 12 x 12 inches. Copyright © 2000 Peter Sís. Reprinted with permission from Farrar, Straus, Giroux Books for Young Readers. All rights reserved.

Page 42: "Float." ***Ballerina!*** (Greenwillow Books). Pen and ink and watercolor on paper. 5 x 5 inches. Copyright © 2001 Peter Sís. Used by permission of HarperCollins Publishers.

Page 43: Illustration for page 11. ***Ship Ahoy!*** (Greenwillow Books). Pen and ink and watercolor on paper. 8 x 8 inches. Copyright © 1999 Peter Sís.

Page 44: "How do we know this king exists?" ***The Conference of the Birds*** (The Penguin Press). Pen and ink on paper. 14 x 21 inches. Copyright © 2011 Peter Sís. Used by permission of Penguin Press, an imprint of Penguin Publishing Group, a division of Penguin Random House LLC. All rights reserved.

Page 45: Cover illustration. ***The Conference of the Birds*** (The Penguin Press). Gesso and gold acrylic on painted wood case cover. 9 x 5 x 1/4 inches. Copyright © 2011 Peter Sís. Used by permission of Penguin Press, an imprint of Penguin Publishing Group, a division of Penguin Random House LLC. All rights reserved.

Page 46: Sketchbook pages. ***Robinson*** (Scholastic Press). Pen and ink and watercolor on paper. 12 x 18 inches (open). Copyright © 2017 Peter Sís. Courtesy of Scholastic Inc.

Page 47: "Is there no one here but me?" ***Robinson*** (Scholastic Press). Pen and ink and watercolor on paper. 12 x 20 inches. Copyright © 2017 Peter Sís. Courtesy of Scholastic Inc.

Page 48: ***I Am a Man,*** tapestry design celebrating Martin Luther King Jr. commissioned by Art for Amnesty, Amnesty International, 2017. Pen and ink and watercolor on paper. 12 x 8 inches. Copyright © Peter Sís.

EXHIBITION CHECKLIST

An asterisk* denotes the work is illustrated.
Unless otherwise noted, all works by Peter Sís (American, born in Czechoslovakia, 1949) and from the collection of the artist.

JOURNEY: A LIFE IN PICTURES

The Three Golden Keys (Doubleday, 1994)

*"There was nobody anywhere." Pen and ink, oil pastel, and gold leaf on paper. 13 x 21 inches.

"I follow my cat for a long time." Pen and ink, oil pastel, and gold leaf on paper. 13 x 21 inches.

"Other characters emerge from the rows of books." Pen and ink, oil pastel, and gold leaf on paper. 13 x 21 inches.

"When I stumble out of the library, the cat is waiting to lead me on." Pen and ink, oil pastel, and gold leaf on paper. 13 x 21 inches.

"The garden has turned into the Emperor's court!" Pen and ink, oil pastel, and gold leaf on paper. 13 x 21 inches.

*"I follow the determined cat back across the ancient bridge." Pen and ink, oil pastel, and gold leaf on paper. 13 x 21 inches.

"And then I am back in the winding streets of childhood . . ." Pen and ink, oil pastel, gold leaf, and gesso on paper. 13 x 21 inches.

Illustration for ***Ship Ahoy!*** (Greenwillow Books, 1999)

"How do we know this king exists?" *The Conference of the Birds* (The Penguin Press, 2011)

Tibet: Through the Red Box
(Frances Foster Books, 1998)

"The red box is on the table, waiting." Pen and ink, watercolor, and gold leaf on paper. 10 x 20 inches.

*"Sick for a few weeks after getting lost in a snowstorm...." Pen and ink, watercolor, and gold leaf on paper. 17 x 17 inches.

"Potala." Pen and ink, watercolor, and gold leaf on paper. 16 x 16 inches.

*"He stumbled into a red room . . ." Pen and ink, watercolor, and gold leaf on paper. 16 x 16 inches.

"Next he came to a green room, square and circular, ear of the earth." Pen and ink, oil pastel, watercolor, gold leaf, and gesso on paper. 16 x 16 inches.

"After that he entered a blue room, frozen in light and dark, eye of the soul." Pen and ink, watercolor, and gold acrylic on paper. 16 x 16 inches.

"And at last a deep, dark room." Pen and ink, watercolor, gold leaf, and gesso on paper. 16 x 16 inches.

*"I hear the deep voice of my father." Pen and ink, watercolor, gold acrylic, and gesso on paper. 10 x 20 inches.

The Wall: Growing Up Behind the Iron Curtain (Frances Foster Books, 2007)

*Sketchbook. Various materials. 12 x 9 inches (closed).

"Then he drew people." Pen and black and red ink on paper. 14 x 10 inches.

". . . he drew what he was told to at school." Pen and black and red ink on paper. 14 3/4 x 10 inches.

"Then he found out there were things he wasn't told." Pen and black and red ink on paper. 14 x 10 inches.

"This was the time of brainwashing." Pen and ink and watercolor on paper. 15 x 22 inches.

*"It was the Prague Spring of 1968!" Pen and ink and watercolor on paper. 14 x 21 inches.

*"Everyone wanted to draw." Pen and ink and colored pencil on paper. 14 x 10 inches.

*"They painted a wall filled with their dreams and repainted it again and again." Pen and ink and colored pencil on paper. 14 x 10 inches.

*"He dreamed of being free." Pen and ink and colored pencil on paper. 12 x 18 inches.

Illustration for pages 46–47. Pen and ink and watercolor on paper. 14 x 21 inches.

*"Sometimes dreams come true." Pen and ink and watercolor on paper. 12 x 18 inches.

ADVENTURERS, SCIENTISTS, AND HEROES: PICTURE-BOOK BIOGRAPHIES

Follow the Dream: The Story of Christopher Columbus (Alfred A. Knopf, 1991)

"He dreamed of the faraway places and people...." Pen and ink, oil pastel, gold leaf, and gesso on paper. 15 x 14 inches.

"Fulfilling his dream was not easy." Pen and ink, oil pastel, gold leaf, and gesso on paper. 10 x 23 inches.

*"Then, on the seventy-first day, a little piece of land appeared on the horizon." Pen and ink, oil pastel, gold leaf, and gesso on paper. 20 x 26 inches.

"Columbus had a second audience with the King and Queen . . ." Pen and ink, oil pastel, gold leaf, and gesso on paper. 15 x 17 inches.

"Six years later, Christopher Columbus was still the only one to believe that land lay to the west . . ." Pen and ink, oil pastel, gold leaf, and gesso on paper. 15 x 17 inches.

"The three ships headed west...." Pen and ink, oil pastel, gold leaf, and gesso on paper. 15 x 17 inches.

"But from the beginning the crew was uneasy." Pen and ink, oil pastel, gold leaf, and gesso on paper. 15 x 17 inches.

A Small Tall Tale from the Far Far North (Alfred A. Knopf, 1993)

Cover illustration. Pen and ink and watercolor on paper. 11 x 23 inches.

*"I hear voices, as in a dream." Pen and ink and watercolor on paper. 9 x 21 inches.

"The Eskimos surrounded me with a trusting friendliness." Pen and ink and watercolor on paper. 9 x 21 inches.

Starry Messenger: Galileo Galilei (Frances Foster Books, 1996)

*Cover illustration. Pen and ink and watercolor on paper. 13 x 20 inches.

Endpapers illustrations. Pen and ink, watercolor, and gold acrylic on paper. 12 x 18 inches.

"Night after night, he gazed through his telescope . . ." Pen and ink and watercolor on paper. 11 x 13 inches.

*"He was tired in the Pope's court, and everyone could see the stars had left his eyes." Pen and ink and watercolor on paper. 11 x 13 inches.

"Galileo was condemned to spend the rest of his life locked in his house under guard." Pen and ink, watercolor, and gold acrylic on paper. 11 x 13 inches.

The Tree of Life: A Book Depicting the Life of Charles Darwin, Naturalist, Geologist, & Thinker (Frances Foster Books, 2003)

*"Dr. Darwin wants the best for his children." Pen and ink and watercolor on paper. 11 x 13 inches.

*"When Charles is nine, his father send him to join his brother at the nearby boarding school." Pen and ink and watercolor on paper. 10 x 10 inches.

"When Charles returns home from Wales, a letter from Professor Henslow awaits him . . ." Pen and ink and watercolor on paper. 10 x 10 inches.

*"The Voyage of The Beagle." Pen and ink and watercolor on paper. 14 x 21 inches.

"On the Origin of Species sparked an explosion." Pen and ink and watercolor on paper. 14 x 21 inches.

"On the Origin of Species." Pen and ink and watercolor on paper. 12 x 17 inches.

The Conference of the Birds (The Penguin Press, 2011)

*Sketchbook. Various materials. 11 x 8 inches (closed).

*Cover illustration. Gesso and gold acrylic on painted wood case cover. 9 x 5 x $^1/_4$ inches.

*"How do we know this king exists?" Pen and ink on paper. 14 x 21 inches.

*Illustration for pages 64–65. Pen and ink on paper. 12 x 18 inches.

"The Valley of Love." Pen and ink and watercolor on paper. 12 x 18 inches.

"The Valley of Unity." Pen and ink and watercolor on paper. 12 x 18 inches.

Illustration for pages 126–127. Pen and ink, watercolor, and gold acrylic on paper. 12 x 18 inches.

The Pilot and the Little Prince: The Life of Antoine de Saint-Exupéry (Frances Foster Books, 2014)

Cover illustration. Pen and ink and watercolor on paper. 12 x 19 inches.

*Illustration for pages 16–17. Pen and ink and watercolor on paper. 13 x 19 inches.

"Being a pioneer air mail pilot was everything Antoine dreamed it would be." Pen and ink, watercolor, and gold acrylic on paper. 12 x 18 inches.

"Eventually, Antoine returned to France." Pen and ink on paper. 12 x 18 inches.

"The plane was destroyed but the two men were not hurt." Pen and ink and watercolor on paper. 18 x 12 inches.

*"From the skies, Antoine watched the fires, smoke, and destruction the Germans left . . ." Pen and ink and watercolor on paper. 12 x 18 inches.

"But he never returned." Pen and ink and watercolor on paper. 18 x 12 inches.

Robinson (Scholastic Press, 2017)

Sketchbook. Various materials. 11 x 7 inches (closed).

*Sketchbook. Various materials. 9 x 12 inches (closed).

Thumbnail sketches. Pen and ink and watercolor on paper. 14 x 17 inches.

Cover illustration. Pen and ink and watercolor on paper. 14 x 10 inches.

Cover illustration for *The Conference of the Birds* (The Penguin Press, 2011)

"My friends and I love adventure." Pen and ink and watercolor on paper. 12 x 20 inches.

"Mom takes me home and tucks me into bed." Pen and ink and watercolor on paper. 12 x 20 inches.

*"Is there no one here but me?" Pen and ink and watercolor on paper. 12 x 20 inches.

"The animals here are kind." Pen and ink and watercolor on paper. 12 x 19 inches.

*"I invite them to my table and we celebrate the harvest." Pen and ink and watercolor on paper. 12 x 20 inches.

"I feel stronger now and brave." Pen and ink and watercolor on paper. 12 x 20 inches.

Forthcoming book on Nicholas Winton (unfinished).
*Sketchbook, 2018. Various materials. 12 x 9 inches (closed).

Kristallnacht, 2019. Scratchboard. 12 x 9 inches.

Forthcoming illustrations. Various materials. Various dimensions.

DINOSAURS AND DANCERS: BOOKS FOR YOUNG READERS

Rainbow Rhino (Alfred A. Knopf, 1987)
*"They told one another stories, and they took long walks together." Pen and ink, oil pastel, and gesso on board. 11 x 16 inches.

"'What a beautiful lake!' Said the blue bird." Pen and ink, oil pastel, and gesso on board. 10 x 16 inches.

Waving (Greenwillow Books, 1988)
"9 Girl Scouts waved at the school children." Pen and ink and watercolor on paper. 9 x 18 inches.

An Ocean World (Greenwillow Books, 1992)
Illustration for page 11. Pen and ink and watercolor on paper. 11 x 15 inches.

*Illustration for page 17. Pen and ink and watercolor on paper. 11 x 15 inches.

Illustration for page 21. Pen and ink and watercolor on paper. 11 x 15 inches.

Komodo! (Greenwillow Books, 1993)
"I have loved dragons as long as I can remember." Pen and ink and watercolor on paper. 10 x 15 inches.

"Then it was gone. Or was it?" Pen and ink and watercolor on paper. 11 x 16 inches.

Fire Truck (Greenwillow Books, 1998)
"He drove around his neighborhood with sirens blaring." Watercolor on paper. 9 x 17 inches.

Sketchbook pages for ***Robinson*** (Scholastic Press, 2017)

Trucks, Trucks, Trucks (Greenwillow Books, 1999)
"Lifting." Watercolor on paper. 21 x 8 inches.

Ship Ahoy! (Greenwillow Books, 1999)
*Illustration for page 11. Pen and ink and watercolor on paper. 8 x 8 inches.

Madlenka (Frances Foster Books, 2000)
Madlenka dummy book series, 1996. Various materials. 3 x 4 x 4 inches.

*"Hey everyone . . . my tooth is loose!" Pen and ink and watercolor on paper. 14 x 13 inches.

"Jumping with joy, she skips down the street and sees her friend Mr. Gaston, the French baker." Pen and ink and watercolor on paper. 14 x 13 inches.

*"France." Pen and ink and pastel on paper. 12 x 25 inches.

*"India." Pen and ink, watercolor, and gold acrylic on paper. 12 x 12 inches.

"Italy." Pen and ink and watercolor on paper. 12 x 12 inches.

"Germany." Pen and ink and oil pastel on paper. 14 x 26 inches.

Dinosaur! (Greenwillow Books, 2000)
Illustration for pages 20–21. Pen and ink and watercolor on paper. 10 x 20 inches.

Ballerina! (Greenwillow Books, 2001)
"Stretch." Pen and ink and watercolor on paper. 5 x 5 inches.

"Twirl." Pen and ink and watercolor on paper. 5 x 5 inches.

*"Float." Pen and ink and watercolor on paper. 5 x 5 inches.

Madlenka's Dog (Frances Foster Books, 2002)
Cover illustration. Pen and ink and watercolor on paper. 12 x 12 inches.

*Illustration for pages 24–25. Pen and ink and watercolor on paper. 9 x 19 inches.

Illustration for pages 26–27. Pen and ink and watercolor on paper. 9 x 19 inches.

The Train of States (Greenwillow Books, 2004)
*"Massachusetts." Pen and ink and watercolor on paper. 11 x 13 inches.

"Maryland." Pen and ink and watercolor on paper. 11 x 13 inches.

Play, Mozart, Play! (Greenwillow Books, 2006)
"Mozart played in London and Amsterdam and Paris." Pen and ink and watercolor on paper. 12 x 22 inches.

*"Mozart played for kings and princes and dukes, and queens and one empress and one pope." Pen and ink and watercolor on paper. 12 x 22 inches.

"Is there no one here but me?" ***Robinson*** (Scholastic Press, 2017)

"Wolfgang Amadeus Mozart lived a long time ago."
Pen and ink and watercolor on paper.
12 x 22 inches.

Madlenka Soccer Star (Frances Foster Books, 2010)
Illustration for pages 27–28. Pen and ink and watercolor on paper.
10 x 19 inches.

Ice Cream Summer (Scholastic Press, 2015)
"I write a lot." Pen and ink and watercolor on paper. 8 x 16 inches.

ART IN PUBLIC PLACES

**Manhattan Whale*, poster design commissioned by Arts for Transit, Metropolitan Transportation Authority, New York City, 2001. Pen and ink, watercolor, and gold acrylic on paper. 8 x 43 inches.

Happy City, glass mosaic design for 86th Street and Lexington station commissioned by Metropolitan Transportation Authority, New York City, 2003. Pen and ink and watercolor on paper. 12 x 26 inches.

Flying Man, tapestry design honoring Czech Republic President Václav Havel commissioned by Václav Havel Airport Prague, 2011. Pen and ink and watercolor on paper. 13 x 11 inches.

Yellow Submarine, tapestry design celebrating John Lennon, 2016. Pen and ink, watercolor, and gold acrylic on paper. 7 x 18 inches.

**I Am a Man*, tapestry design celebrating Martin Luther King Jr. commissioned by Art for Amnesty, Amnesty International, 2017. Pen and ink and watercolor on paper. 12 x 8 inches.

INDEPENDENT ART

Evelyn, 1980. Oil and gesso on egg shell. 2 x 1 inches.

"From the cauldron of literature: an exile's journal," editorial drawing for *The New York Times Book Review*, 1988. Pen and ink on paper. 3 x 4 inches.

Columbus, 1991. Oil, gesso, and gold acrylic on paper and egg shell. 2 x 1 inches.

"The opera is comic, the blood is real," editorial drawing for *The New York Times Book Review*, 1991. Pen and ink on paper. 6 x 7 inches.

"Outwaiting time on the Dordogne," editorial drawing for *The New York Times Book Review*, 1992. Pen and ink on paper. 5 x 11 inches.

"Good enough for her mother's mother's mother," editorial drawing for *The New York Times Book Review*, 1993. Pen and ink on paper. 3 x 11 inches.

Cat Woman, 1995. Oil, gesso, and gold acrylic on paper and egg shell. 2 x 1 inches.

Terry's Chores, 2008. Gouache, gold, and oil pastel on washboard. 22 x 12 x 1 inches.

Magic Potion, 2010. Brown ink on gold labels on bottles found at house of Washington Irving. Various dimensions. Letter to Olive, 2018. Pen and ink on paper. 11 x 8 7/16 inches.

I Am a Man, tapestry design celebrating Martin Luther King Jr. commissioned by Art for Amnesty, Amnesty International, 2017